W9-BST-796

Special Thanks

to

Tana Pearson

for her clerical help

Contents

Active Games

Psychiatry

Select four or five people from the group to be "psychiatrists" and send them out of the room. The remaining members of the group choose one person to be the "patient." Each person assumes the characteristics of the person on her/his right. For example, if asked the color of the "patient's" hair, the person questioned would say "blonde" if that is the hair color of the person on his right. Bring in "psychiatrists" one at a time. "Psychiatrists" may ask any question of any person except the name of the "patient." Game continues until all "psychiatrists" have identified the "patient."

Pantomime

Each player picks out a scene to pantomime. It can be a Bible scene, commercial, old proverb, etc. The one who guesses the scene gets to act out the next scene.

Predicaments

One person leaves the room while the others select a predicament, such as "in the shower and the doorbell rings, then the telephone rings", or "out of gas in a rainstorm." The person returns and tries to learn the nature of the predicament. To do so he asks the players in turn, "What would you do in this predicament?" and each must give an appropriate answer. The one who gives the predicament away is the next to leave the room.

Compare It to Me

While one player is out of the room, the others choose an object in plain sight. The player returns and goes up to the others in turn, saying "Compare it to me." The person then makes a comparison between the player and the object. When the person guesses the object, the person who gave the last comparison must take the player's place.

Guessing Proverbs

One player leaves the room while the others agree on a well-known proverb. The player returns and asks questions of the others. Each one addressed must answer the question put to him, and his reply must include one word of the selected proverb, the words following in order; that is, first word of the proverb and so on. The one who gives the proverb away is next.

Posing

Two or more people stand with their back to the group. A pose is described and they turn to face the group and assume the pose immediately. Examples: Girl seeing mouse, child taking medicine, learning to water-ski, playing soccer.

Balloon Bump

Each person is given a balloon to tie around his/her waist so that the balloon is in back. The object of the game is to break balloons by bumping into one another. The one who survives with an unbroken balloon is the winner.

Button Snap

Draw a starting line and a goal line. Place a button for each player on the starting line. Also give each player a button. Players press the edge of their button against the other button to make it fly a distance. If the button leaves the game area, it is returned to the starting line. The player whose button reaches the finish line first is the winner.

Bow Tie Relay

Form two sides, giving the first player of each side an old bow tie. At a given signal the first player ties it in a bow around the neck of the second player. The second player unties it and ties it around the neck of the third player. This continues until one side wins.

Potato Race

Form two teams and have the players seated. Start a potato relay at the beginning of each side. The potato must be passed with the two feet. If the potato should hit the floor, it is brought back to the first person and started again.

Paper Duel

The players are paired off and blindfolded. Each duelist is given a tightly rolled newspaper as a weapon to be held in the right hand. The left hand grasps one end of a yard stick. Being unable to see, the blows to the enemy are not too accurate. Allow four minutes and then choose another pair.

Bottle the Pins

Provide a small-mouth half-gallon jar and ten clothespins. Let each person drop the pins into the bottle one at a time. The one who drops in the most is the winner.

Annie Oakley

Line three boys in a row. About six feet opposite them, line three girls in a row. Each boy holds a small paper cup on the top of his head. Each girl is given a water gun and she tries to put as much water as possible into the cup.

Egghead

This game is for boys and requires cooperation and ingenuity. Divide the group into pairs. Establish a starting and a finishing line. The smaller boy gets on the shoulders of the larger boy. The first pair to reach the goal are the winners. The snag in this game is that the person who does the walking is blindfolded, and the rider has an egg in his mouth.

Gum Animals

Each person is given a piece of gum and told to start chewing until further orders. After a while give each a toothpick and a small piece of cardboard with the name of an animal written on it. Each player then molds his gum with his toothpick into the shape of the animal written on the cardboard. When all have finished, display each and choose the winner.

In the Ring

Draw a ring on the floor large enough for the men of the party to stand inside and still leave a margin of three feet. The men stay inside the ring with arms folded, facing the center. When a signal is given, all begin to push and shove the others out, while trying to remain inside the ring themselves. Anyone who is pushed over the line or unfolds his arms is out of the game. The shoving continues until one player remains.

Toothpicks

Scatter a box of toothpicks on the floor and see who can pick up the most toothpicks in a given time. After all the excitement, count the picks and reward the winner.

Walking on Eggs

Except for one person, all participants should be sent from the room. Place a number of eggs on the floor and tell this player to note their location. Blindfold him while someone else quickly and quietly picks up the eggs. The blindfolded person is instructed to walk through the eggs without stepping on any. When the blindfold is removed, he can see why all the merriment. Continue calling in players one by one.

Conversation

Let each boy choose the subject of discourse. A girl should then talk to him on this subject for one minute. Then the girl next in line becomes his partner. When each girl has talked to every boy, the boys vote on the ability of the speaker. Then vice versa.

Tomato Game

Divide the group into couples. Put a tomato between the boy's and the girl's forehead. The boy then carefully takes off his shoe and the girl must put the shoe on her foot and tie it without dropping the tomato. The first couple to complete the maneuvers without mishap wins.

Horseplay

Have four boys pretend to be horses by getting down on all fours. Choose five girls to be cowgirls. Play music and when it stops the cowgirls jump on the horses. The girl left standing can pull and tug trying to get the others off. Poor horses!!!

Picking Noses

This game is for married couples. Have four women sit down, cover them with a sheet, cut holes in the sheet for their noses to come through. The husbands are then brought out one by one and each picks (locates) his wife's nose. When he thinks he has located it, he kisses the tip of it. After all have finished, the women are uncovered. Roles are then reversed and each woman picks husband's nose.

Hanging Apples

Attach a string to an apple and suspend it from the ceiling. Choose someone to try to bite the apple without using hands or arms. It is nearly impossible. This is a hilarious game but it dies after about the second or third individual.

Elopement Race

This is a race for boy-and-girl pairs. An umbrella and a closed suitcase containing various articles of men's and women's clothing and accessories are placed on the floor a few feet in front of each couple. At the starting signal, each pair rushes to their suitcase, opens it, puts on all the clothing over their clothes, and raises the umbrella. They then remove all the clothing, close the suitcase, close the umbrella, and run to the finish line. (Clothing should be put on over clothing participants are wearing).

Chewing Tug of War

This is a contest for two people. A piece of candy is tied to the middle of a piece of string eight to ten feet long. Each person takes one end of the string in his mouth and clasps his hands behind his back. At a signal, each begins to chew the string into his mouth until one reaches the candy. The person who gets the candy is the winner.

Paper Race

Each person is given two pieces of newspaper (folded twice). The object of the game is to reach the finish line by stepping only on newspapers. This can be done by placing the newspapers on the floor, stepping on them, and then shifting the papers and advancing.

Feather Race

Each person is given a small feather and a fan. The person drives the feather to the finish line and back by fanning it. (A $2'' \times 2''$ square of tissue paper can be used instead of a feather.)

Bean Extracting

Give each person a cup containing several beans to hold in one hand, a teaspoon to hold in the other, and an empty cup to put on top of his head. While looking into a mirror, each player transfers the beans one at a time. The player who completes the task in the shortest time is the winner.

The Lost Child

One player leaves the room, and while she is gone, a second player leaves. The first player is recalled and given ten seconds to discover who is missing.

Balloon Bust

Have all the players tie balloons on their ankles. The object of the game is to burst your opponents' balloons while keeping yours whole.

Stone Face Contest

Two players stand back to back. At a given signal both turn and face each other. They compete to see who can stand longer without laughing. They can make motions, but cannot make sounds or touch each other.

Arranging the Newspaper

One complete newspaper must be prepared for each player. Mix up all the pages. Sitting as close to each other as possible, players must restore their own papers to the original order. This is very difficult in close quarters. The first one to finish is the winner.

Break the Balloon

Divide players into two teams and give each team a chair. All players are given a blown-up balloon and at a given signal each must take his balloon and sit on it to break it. The team who finishes first wins.

Bounce the Ball

Choose as many players as you wish to compete in this game. Place a trash can about eight feet from the players. Each player is then given three tries to bounce a volleyball on the floor so that it lands in the trash can. He scores one point for each successful landing. The player with the most points wins.

Measurements

Lay a boy out on a table and measure him for a new wardrobe. Hold each arm up and measure it. Then hold each leg up and measure. When the second leg is held up, have someone put an ice cube down the pantleg.

Stocking Feet

You will need two or three boys. Have each one put on a pair of rubber gloves. Seat them and have them remove their shoes. After blindfolding them, give each a pair of nylon stockings (not pantyhose). The object of the game is to see which boy can put on the stockings first. (Nylon is very difficult to feel while wearing rubber gloves.)

Goes Together

Write each of the following words on a piece of paper and hand one to every guest. On a given signal, each guest must try to find the word that goes together with his word. You now have partners for another game.

	Partner
Hospital	Doctor
Lock	Key
Shoe	Sock
Glove	Hand
Bullet	Gun
Needle	Thread
Spectacles	Eyes
Soap	Water
Bank	Money
Crime	Jail
Night	Darkness
Romance	Love

Marshmallows

Three couples are needed for this game. The women are blind-folded and each is given a cup of minature marshmallows and a spoon. The three men stand with their hands behind their back. At a given signal, the women proceed to feed the men the marshmallows. It is the man's job to get his mouth to the spoon. The one who eats the most marshmallows is the winner.

Copycat

Send a few people from the room. Prepare two bowls: one with the bottom blackened with a flame, the other with the bottom clean. Bring one person in at a time. Tell him to keep his eyes on you at all times and to do exactly as you do. Make a few movements and then give him the blackened bowl. Rub your hand on the bottom of your bowl and mark your face. When he does this he will be marking his face black. Give him a mirror.

Walking Alphabet

Divide a large group into two teams and pin a letter of the alphabet on the front of every person. Give each side the same letters and have them stand away from each other. A Bible question is then asked that can be answered with the spelling of one or two words. The team that spells it first, by aligning those letters in correct order, gets ten points. Should a team misspell or give the wrong answer, deduct five points from their score.

Books of the Bible

Choose some outstanding Bible incidents in the Old and New Testaments, but not more than one from any book of the Bible. Briefly mention these incidents and see who can tell you the book that contains the story.

We Three Kings

Three or four players are sent from the room. They are brought in one at a time to meet the three kings. The kings are very angry and displeased. The person must get on his knees and bow while addressing them. The leader will introduce the kings to the person. The first king is Owa, the second king is Tagoo, the third king is Siam. The only thing that will please the mean kings is to repeat their names, first louder, then faster. Finally it will dawn on the person that he is saying, "O what a goose I am."

Jar Ring Toss

Prepare a 28″ square board by driving twenty-three 3″ nails into it at an angle. Hang the board on the wall or stand it on a table at shoulder height. Give the player ten rings, and have him stand ten feet from the board and throw the rings. For added interest, give the rings different point values. Keep score.

Burst the Balloons

Divide into two groups. Put two straight chairs in the middle of the room. Select a person to stand behind each chair and place balloons on the seat. The object of the game is to see which group can burst all their balloons first. As each player bursts his balloon, he quickly moves out of the way for the next person. One balloon will be filled with water. Pick a good sport to break that balloon.

Banana Race

Give each player a banana with the instructions to peel and eat it while holding one hand behind him. On a given signal, they begin. The first one who finishes and whistles is the winner.

Balloon Instructions

Divide the group into two teams and give each player a balloon. Inside every balloon is a small slip of paper with the same written instructions. The object of the game is to see which group can first complete the tasks of blowing up their balloons, popping them, reading the instructions, and carrying out the instructions. (Create your own instructions.)

Huff and Puff

Establish the goal line and the starting line. Give everyone a balloon. They are to blow up their balloons, get on their hands and knees and blow their balloons to the goal line without touching them. The first to accomplish this is the winner.

Chinese Get Up

Have all the men sit on the floor with their arms folded across their chests. At the given signal they are to get up without uncrossing their arms.

Throwing Contest

Choose the strongest in the group to participate in this game. Line them up and give each a paper plate. All get three tries to throw the plate. The one who throws it the farthest is the winner.

Egg-Cracking Contest

Give everyone a hard-boiled egg and instruct them to hold the small end up. Invite the players to challenge each other to egg-cracking duels. In a duel, two players hold out their eggs and flick the end of their opponent's egg with their finger. The person whose egg remains uncracked wins his opponent's egg. The other person is out. Any eggs accumulated before a person goes out may be kept; he need only give up the one egg. The game ends when only one person is left standing. There are

18

two winners: the one whose egg remains uncracked, and the one who has collected the most eggs.

Fanning

Divide your group into two teams and ask each team to form into a circle. Place a pie tin in the middle of each circle. In one circle scatter thirty white tissue hearts, in the other scatter thirty red tissue hearts. Give each player a paper plate. Begin. The team who fans the most hearts into the tin is the winner. (Allow five to ten minutes.)

Ring the Bell

Cut the center from a paper ornament (make it seasonal such as a pumpkin or valentine) and attach a small bell to the center. Hang the ornament from the ceiling. Divide the group into two teams and give each person a chance to ring the bell by throwing a small bean bag. The team that rings the bell the most is the winner.

Nut-Throwing Contest

Put a small bowl inside a large bowl and place the two bowls in a dishpan. Each player then tries to throw three nuts into the small bowl. The player scores five points for each nut that lands in the small bowl, three points for each nut that lands in the large bowl, and one point for each that lands in the dishpan.

Cities

Prepare a card for every letter of the alphabet. The leader holds up one card. The first person to call out the name of a city beginning with that letter receives the card. The cards can be held up in any order. At the end of the game, the person with the most cards is the winner.

States and Capitals

Form two teams with an equal number of players on each team. One team is assigned states and the other capitals. The "state" team names a state and the "capital" team must give the capital. Then the "capital" team names a capital and the "state" team must give the state. For every correct answer give five points. For every incorrect answer take away ten points. Reverse the state and capital assignments.

Name that Tune

Group all players into pairs. One pair plays at a time. They are seated in chairs side by side. Place a bell a short distance away. When the music starts the first one to run and ring the bell and name the tune is the winner. Give each pair three tries. After each pair has had a turn, let the winners play against each other.

Sonny Boy

The leader begins this game with a statement like, "Sonny Boy is funny and looney but not crazy. He likes moo cows but not milk cows." Each person is given a chance to make a statement about Sonny Boy, but the leader will have to judge whether he's telling the truth. His words must have double letters in them to be acceptable. The game continues until most (or all) of the people catch on.

Clumsy Wrestler

Boys usually like this game. Divide the boys into pairs according to size. Have two boys stand facing each other with hands on the other's shoulders. Place a Coke bottle on the floor between them. The boys pull and push to get their opponent to knock over the bottle. The one to knock over the bottle is the loser. Winners may then play against each other.

Chicken Yard Fight

Draw a circle on the ground. Have two players stand inside it each holding his ankles. At a given signal, each player tries to push the other from the circle or make him lose his balance. The first player to release his ankles, leave the circle, or fall, is the loser.

Dressmakers

Divide the group into pairs. Give each pair several newspapers and pins. Each pair has a dressmaker and a model. The dressmaker creates his own style by using his and the model's imagination. Vote to choose the most attractive style.

Tick-Tack-Toe

Create a tick-tack-toe square by using nine chairs. Boys and girls play against each other. The object of the game is to form a row of either three boys or three girls. A girl gets the first chance to choose a seat, a boy follows. Continue to alternate until either an all-boy or all-girl vertical, horizontal, or diagonal line is formed. Play several times.

Guess the Objects

Choose three or four people to participate in this game. Send them out of the room and bring them back in one at a time, blindfolded. Each one is given about eight to ten objects to guess. Make them as eerie to feel as possible. For instance; ice, peeled grapes, chestnut burrs, oysters, etc. The objects may be held for only a moment.

Hit and Miss

Choose someone to be "it." Have her stand with her back to the group. A towel with a knot tied in it is passed from one person to another until someone throws it to "it" and hits her. She then turns quickly and tries to guess who hit her. If she misses, the game continues. If she guesses correctly, that person takes her place.

Fill in the Blank

Send one player out of the room. The other players decide on a word that has a double meaning and spelling, such as "write." When the player returns to the game the others start a conversation, substituting the word *blank* when they need to use the agreed-on word. The person who makes the last statement before the player guesses the word leaves the room.

Crazy Gifts

Ask everyone to bring a wrapped gift to the party. The gift should be something useless or of no value to the person. When each person arrives, put his name on a piece of paper and put it in a bowl. When all are present, draw two names at once. These two people are to exchange gifts. Do only two at a time so all may enjoy each gift.

Balance

Have someone stand with his heels against the wall. Place a coin eighteen inches in front of his toes. He is to bend over, get the coin, and stand back up, without losing his balance.

Pantomime Rhymes

The leader chooses two words that rhyme. He then says, for example, 'I'm thinking of a word that rhymes with look." Any player may then say, "Is it _____?" Instead of saying the word, the player must pantomime it. He may, for instance, pretend to be reading a book. The leader then says, "No, it is not book." Or, "Yes, it is book." The person who guesses correctly becomes the leader. Only one-syllable words may be used.

Adjectives

Have each player write an adjective and his name on a slip of paper. Collect the papers and give them to someone who will make up a story using the adjectives coupled with the names. For example, "One day skinny Dorothy and fat Bob went into the woods to pick flowers. As they walked along a dark path they heard screaming. They ran and found silly Steve sitting on a tree branch and gorgeous Vicki chasing a mouse away from the tree." Choose an imaginative storyteller to present the story.

Egg Toss

Have two players stand facing each other about three feet apart. Give a raw egg to one of the players. He throws it to his partner. If his partner catches the egg without breaking it, the players each take a large step backward. For every accurate catch the players get to take another step backward. If the egg cracks or hits the ground, the couple is eliminated. Several couples may compete to see who can stay in the game the longest.

Raw Egg Relay

Divide a group into two equal teams. Line them up. Place a pot of water containing a raw egg for every player a few feet in front of the first person in each team. Give each team a spoon. At a given signal, the first player gets an egg out of the pot with the spoon and takes it to an egg carton some distance away. If she should drop the egg, she is to clean it up before the next person on her team may proceed. The team filling up their carton first is the winner.

Life Saver Relay

Divide a group into two teams. Give everyone a toothpick to hold between their teeth. Place a Life Saver on the toothpick of the first person on each side. The game begins. The Life Saver is passed from person to person by lining up the toothpicks so that the Life Saver slides onto the next person's toothpick. Hands may not be used. Should a Life Saver drop, that team begins again with the first person and a new Life Saver. The first team to relay a Life Saver to the end of its line is the winner.

Slap Tag

All players stand in a circle clasping hands. "It" runs around the outside of the circle and tags a player as he runs. The person tagged immediately runs in the opposite direction from "it." Both try to reach the vacant spot first. The successful runner rejoins the circle, and the unsuccessful runner becomes "it."

Two Deep

The players, except two, stand in a circle. One of the players is the runner, the other is the chaser. The chaser pursues the runner around the circle. The runner saves himself from being tagged by stepping in front of one of the players in the circle. That player becomes the runner and the chaser attempts to tag him. Whenever the runner is tagged, he becomes the new chaser and the game continues.

Who Is the Leader?

The players form a circle. One person leaves the room while the group chooses a leader. The leader begins an action, such as clapping. The person is brought back into the room to stand in the middle of the circle. The leader carefully changes the action and the other players follow suit. The person in the center tries to discover who the leader is. It is important that the other players not give away the leader by watching her too closely. When the leader is discovered, she leaves the room and a new leader is appointed.

Number Exchange

All players sit in chairs placed in a circle. The players number off consecutively. One player stands in the center. He calls two numbers. Those persons whose numbers were called must quickly change places. While they do so, the center player tries to reach one of their places first. The person left without a place becomes the center player. After a time, the center player may call more than two numbers, or he may call "number exchange" and everyone must exchange seats.

Rhythm

Players sit in a circle and take consecutive numbers. A rhythm is established, such as tap knees twice, clap hands twice, snap the right fingers and then the left fingers. One person begins by calling his number on the first snap and someone else's number on the second snap. The person whose number is called must repeat his own number on the first snap and another person's number on the second snap. Anyone who breaks the rhythm is eliminated.

Kangaroo

All players form a circle and stoop down. The first person says to the next, "Do you know how to play 'Kangaroo'?" The player says "No" and asks the next player. This continues on around the circle until it reaches the first player again who says, "Well then, what are we doing in this silly position?"

The Winker

Arrange enough chairs in a circle to seat all of the girls in the group. Leave one chair empty. A boy stands behind every chair with hands at his side. The boy behind the empty chair is the "winker." He must find a girl to fill his chair. To do so, he winks at a girl and she must slip away before the boy behind her puts his hand on her shoulder. Should she escape, her boy becomes the "winker" and must fill his chair.

Lost Lover

Teenagers enjoy this game. Seat players in a circle. A blind-folded person stands in the middle. He gropes around until he finds a lap to sit on. He then asks that player, "Are you my lost love?" The player answers in a disguised voice. The blindfolded person gets one chance to guess the identity of the person. If he guesses correctly, he or she becomes the next center person. If the blindfolded person guesses incorrectly, he may sit in another person's lap.

Alphabet Face

Seat players in a circle. Going through the alphabet beginning with "a," one person after another chooses an adjective that begins with that letter to describe his neighbor's face. The first player, for example, turns to the second and says, "You have an adorable face." The second player then turns to the third player and uses an adjective beginning with "b." Continue around the circle as often as you like. No adjectives may be used twice. Anyone who cannot think of an adjective is eliminated.

Chit Chat

Players form a double circle facing each other, boys in the outer circle, girls in the inner circle. At the given signal, the inner circle starts walking. When a signal is given the girls stop and begin to chat with the boy they are facing until a signal is given to start walking again. It is good to assign topics for chit chat, and it is good to have frequent and brief stops.

Couple Run

Divide into couples and form a circle with couples standing side by side. Join hands. One couple is "it." They run around the outside of the circle holding hands, then split the hands of a couple and continue running. The second couple joins hands and begins running in the opposite direction. The first couple to reach the vacant spot remains in the circle, and the other couple becomes "it."

Buzz

The players form a circle and begin counting consecutively. Whenever a number containing a seven or a number divisible by seven is reached, the player must say "buzz" instead of the number. Those who say the number instead of "buzz" are disqualified. The game ends when only one person remains.

Going to the Beach

The leader chooses one or two others to know the object of this game. The group forms a circle. The leader begins by saying, "We're going to the beach. What will you bring? I'm bringing a ___." Proceed around the circle. The leader decides whether or not an item may be brought to the beach; to be acceptable an item must begin with the first letter of the player's first or last name. The game continues until someone (or everyone) guesses the object of the game.

Jack Sprat

All players, except Jack Sprat, form pairs and stand in a circle. Jack gives orders such as "face to face," "back to back," or "side to side." The group follows orders. If Jack should say "Jack Sprat," everyone, including himself, tries for a new partner. The one left without a partner becomes Jack Sprat and the game continues.

Fruit Basket Turn Over

Seat players in a circle. One person stands in the center. Each player is given the name of a fruit. The person in the middle calls out the names of two fruits. The two must quickly change seats. The person in the middle also tries to reach one of the seats. The person left standing then calls out the names of two other fruits. He or she may also call "fruit basket turn over" and everyone must change seats.

Barnyard Upset

This is played just like Fruit Basket Turn Over, except each player is given the name of an animal. When "barnyard upset" is called everyone changes seats.

Hot Breath

Seat everyone in a circle. The leader blindfolds a person, makes him stand, and turns him around several times. The blindfolded person then tries to blow out a lighted candle held by the leader. When he succeeds, the person on his right takes a turn.

Spin the Question

Seat the players in a circle. One person, the spinner, sits in the center. The spinner spins a Coke bottle while asking a question. When the bottle stops, the person it points to must answer the question. This may continue as long as you like. The success of this game depends on the creativity of the questions.

If You Can Do This

Two people need to know the object of this game. The leader begins by clearing his throat. He then makes several movements with a broom while saying, "If you can do this like I can do this, then you can do this like me." He then lets several people try to imitate him, followed by the other person aware of the object of the game (i.e., to begin by clearing one's throat). The game continues until someone (or everyone) catches on.

Ha Ha Game

Divide the players into two teams and seat them in rows facing each other. Toss up an old shoe. When the shoe lands on the floor the side it points to must begin laughing, while the other side must remain grave. If the laughing side can make any of their opponents laugh they gain them on their side. This continues until all players are on one side or until the group tires of it.

Sit-Down Volleyball

Drop the net lower than usual. Have all players sit in straight chairs. Follow the rules for volleyball. All must remain seated except to change seats.

Groups

Have cards with numbers 1, 2, 3, or 4 on them. Give a card to each member of the group, so that there are an equal number of ones, twos, threes, and fours. Then begin to give instructions such as: 1. All threes get into one group. 2. All twos and fours exchange cards. 3. All fours play London Bridge. 4. Everyone get your card initialed by a person with a different number. Make up additional instructions.

Ring on the String

Have a group stand or sit in a circle with one person in the center. Everyone in the circle holds on to a piece of cord with both hands. A ring or safety pin has been placed on the cord and is secretly passed from one person to the next. The person in the middle watches carefully to catch someone in the act of passing. The person caught with the object becomes the middle person.

Alphabet Game

Two or more players are needed for this game. Pick a subject such as cities, men in the Bible, or animals. The first person names a city, for example, that begins with an "a." The players proceed through the alphabet. Anyone who cannot think of a city is eliminated. Continue through the alphabet as often as you like. The person remaining is the winner.

City Exchange

This is played just like Fruit Basket Turn Over (see p. 28) except names of cities are used in the place of fruit. When all are to move the leader calls "city exchange."

This Is My Nose

All players stand in a circle with one person in the center. The center person tells an individual "this is my nose," but touches some other part of his body such as his foot. The player must then touch his nose and say "This is my foot." The object of the game is to do one thing and say another. This continues until someone makes a mistake. That person then enters the center.

Barnyard Talk

Seat everyone in a circle. Go around the circle and whisper in the ear of all but one to be quiet when you ask for barnyard talk. In one person's ear whisper the name of an animal. Tell everyone (aloud) that on the count of three you want to hear barnyard talk and all are to make the sound of their animal. Only one person will make a sound.

Dummy Bag

Have the group sit in a circle and give each person a grocery bag. Tell everyone to put their bag on their head to minimize embarrassment. Tell them to take off one thing they did not wear to bed last night. Some will catch on immediately and remove the bag, others will begin to remove jewelry and clothing. Do not let contestants get carried away with undressing.

Secrets

The players are seated in a circle. Someone whispers a secret to his neighbor, who must then pass it on to his neighbor. When the secret has passed around the circle, the last person to receive it must tell what he heard and the first person must tell what he started. The secret is likely to have changed drastically.

Flying Dutchman

The players stand or sit in a circle with one person, the Flying Dutchman, in the center. A loosely knotted towel is tossed back and forth and the Dutchman tries to intercept it. If he is successful, the one who threw the towel must exchange places with him.

Avoid

Choose a letter of the alphabet to be the unwanted letter. The group forms a semicircle. Establish which end of the semicircle will be the head and which the end. The object of the game is to get to the head of the semicircle. The person at the end begins by asking someone in the semicircle a question. That person must answer the question without using the unwanted letter. If he uses the letter, the last person gets his place and everyone moves down a chair. Move up through the semicircle allowing everyone to ask a question.

Dizzy Stick

One person at a time enters the circle and takes a yardstick. He covers the end of the yardstick with his hands and places his head on his hands. Watching the end of the stick on the floor, he circles the stick six times. He then drops the stick, goes across the room, picks up a book on the floor, and puts the book on a chair. He usually will end up on the floor.

Keepaway

This game is an old favorite. The boys form one team and the girls form another and try to keep the volleyball away from each other.

Sky Ball

Each player numbers off and stands in a circle. The player in the center throws up a volleyball and shouts a number. The person with that number must catch the ball before it hits the ground. If he doesn't he goes to the center.

Imitation

Have the group sit in a circle. Ask for five volunteers and let them each draw a name out of a hat. The names will include people in the group or people from the church. A person who has drawn a name then imitates that person until the group guesses who he is imitating. Let each of the five volunteers have a turn.

Shopping Spree

Have the players sit in a circle. The leader starts the game by saying, "I'm going to Baton Rouge. What shall I buy?" The player to his right must respond with three things that begin with "b" such as bats, balls, and buckets. That player then says, for example, "I'm going to Ragley. What shall I buy?" The person on his right must answer with three things beginning with "r." Continue through the circle. The leader gives each person only to the count of ten to name the three items. If someone fails to name three items he is eliminated.

Orange Pass

Divide the players into two teams. Alternate males and females so that the orange is passed from a male to a female and so on. At a given signal the first person on each team places an orange under his chin and passes it to the next person. Hands may not be used.

Coat and Hat Relay

The players are divided into two teams and each team is given a hat and a coat. At the signal the first person puts on the coat, buttons it, and puts on the hat. He then unbuttons the coat, takes off the hat, and gives them to the next team member. When the last person of a team finishes, he lays the coat and hat in a pile and his team wins.

Clothespin Relay

Divide into two relay teams. Give each team five clothespins. At the signal the first person attaches a clothespin to each finger of one of the second player's hands. The second person then removes them and puts them on the hand of the third person. The last person runs and attaches the clothespins to the first person's hand. The first team to go through the line wins.

Handclasp Relay

Divide a group into two teams. Have the players hold hands and stand in line. At each end of the line is a chair, one of them with ten peanuts (in shells) on it. The peanuts are passed, one at a time, from person to person until they are all transferred to the chair at the far end of the line. The passing must be done with clasped hands.

Nose and Ear Pull

This is a game that takes coordination. It may be performed by one person or by the complete group. The stunt is for the player to cross his left hand over his right and pull his nose and ear. Then he quickly crosses his right hand over his left and pulls his nose and other ear. This will be easy for some and hard for others.

Shopping Relay

Fill two baskets or boxes with identical items (such as screws, hairpins, toothpicks, tacks, and coins). Write the name of one of the items on two slips of paper. Do the same for all the items. Form two equal teams and have them sit on the floor across from each other. The baskets are placed at a distance from the teams. The leader gives the first player of each team two slips of paper that list the same two objects, and so on, so that each player has two slips of paper before you begin. At a given signal the first two players are to go shopping. The players each put on a glove, get their items out of the basket, and give the items to the leader. The players then take off their gloves and run back to give their gloves to the second players. The second players must follow the same procedure. The team to finish first is the winner.

New Fashions

A girl enters the room wearing several "new" fashions. All are instructed to observe her carefully. (She should wear as many articles as possible.) She strolls around for one minute and talks with a few people, then strolls out. Each player must then write down as many of the articles as possible. Score one point for each article correctly listed and subtract two for each one listed incorrectly.

Kaleidoscope

This game may seem easy, but it is really quite difficult. About six players stand in a row in front of the others. The leader assigns each of the six players a color. While the others look away, the six players are rearranged. The others then look at them and try to name their colors.

Memory

A number of articles (not more than ten) are placed on a table in a simple order. Players are given about fifteen seconds to study the articles and then must look away or leave the room. When they return, some of the articles will have been re-arranged. Each player must name the articles that have been moved.

Miss the Bell

A bell is suspended in a hoop about eight or ten inches in diameter. Each player is given a chance to throw a small ball through the hoop. Three points are given for each ball that goes through the hoop without ringing the bell. One point is given if the ball goes through and rings the bell.

Musical Chairs

This game is another old favorite. Count your guests and arrange as many chairs, minus one, in a circle. The guests stand behind the chairs. The music starts, and when it stops all try to get a chair. The person left standing leaves the game and takes a chair with him.

Musical Teams

Divide the players into two teams and have them seated. The pianist plays excerpts of gospel music. The first to stand and name the song earns five points for his team. If someone names the wrong song ten points are deducted from his team's score. If a person guesses five songs he should be asked to sit out and give the others a chance.

Yes and No

Give each guest twenty beans when he arrives. If anyone catches another guest using the words "yes" or "no" at any time during the evening he receives a bean from that person. The guests should be encouraged to mingle and ask questions requiring an answer of yes or no. The one with the most beans at the end of the party is the winner.

Questions

Pin a word to the back of each guest as they arrive. When all have arrived, encourage the guests to ask questions about their words. If anyone should tell another his/her word, both are eliminated from the game. The first person to correctly guess his/her word is the winner.

Valentine Cards

Make an announcement or send out announcements inviting a group to a Valentine party. To be admitted to the party each person must submit a personally made Valentine. A vote should be taken on the cards for beauty and originality.

"I"

Pin a paper heart on each person. Encourage guests to mingle and talk. When someone hears another say the word "I" he gets all the hearts that person is wearing. The person who collects the most hearts wins. This is a good game for Valentine parties.

Matching Shoes

Each girl removes one shoe. All shoes are collected and a shoe is then given to each boy. He is to find the girl it belongs to. They are then partners.

Matching Objects

Two identical sets of objects are prepared. One set is distributed among the girls and the other among the boys. Each player then locates the other player that has the duplicate of his object. The players with the same objects become partners. Use objects such as marbles, flowers, or pictures from magazines.

Match the Cut

Circles, squares, or any shaped object is cut from paper. It is then cut into two parts with one piece given to a boy and another to a girl. The cuts should be irregular, resembling a jigsaw puzzle. The guests find their partners by matching objects, such as, hearts for Valentine's Day, trees for Christmas, turkeys for Thanksgiving, pumpkins for Halloween.

Polaroid Pandemonium

Divide up according to the size of the group and the number of chaperones. Each group is given a Polaroid camera and a list of pictures they are to take. They leave and return when the pictures are taken. The first group back with all the pictures wins. A time limit should be given.

Scavenger Hunt

Divide your group into as many teams as needed. Each captain should be given an identical list of the items to be found. The team that comes back first with all the required items is the winner. Suggested items are: acorns, pinecones, rusty nails, rocks, corn kernels, moss, four-leaf clovers. If cars are used in the hunt, the items listed may be those that require more time or ingenuity to find.

Treasure Hunt

Divide your group into as many teams as needed. Give each team an identical clue written on a piece of paper. This clue should lead the teams to their second clue. All clues should be placed in jars. Instruct the group to take only one clue per team and to leave each jar where they find it. Get permission before placing any containers on private property. Provide adult supervision for each car if your group consists of young people. Continue until all reach a designated spot where a party will be held.

Progressive Supper

If possible, load the complete group on a bus or van. Let the group guess where they will be going. Drive to someone's home for salad. After salad, get back on the bus and drive to a second home for the main course. [Then on to another home for the dessert.] If four homes are available, stop for appetizers or soup.

Password

Divide the group into pairs and seat them facing each other. Give one partner a list of six words beginning with the same letter. At a given signal he is given one minute to go through the list by giving one-word clues to his partner. If his partner cannot guess a word he may go on to the next word. If time allows they may return to a word. Award ten points for each correct answer. If desired, allow the other partner to then give the clues.

Gossip

Players sit in a circle. One begins by whispering, once, a statement to the player on his right. Each player in turn whispers the statement, as he interprets it, to the person on his right.

The last person tells aloud what he heard. The final statement will usually be entirely unlike the original statement.

Getting to Know You Better

Have everyone sit in a circle and promise faithfully to tell the truth. When a statement is read that is true about someone, he must stand. Make up additional statements.

1. You used deodorant today.
2. You brushed your teeth today.
3. You took a bath today.
4. You sang in the tub or shower today.
5. You used hairspray today.
6. You have a runner in your sock.
7. Your socks do not match.
8. You are good-looking but not conceited.
9. You bite your nails.
10. Your fingernails are dirty.
11. You are six feet tall.
12. You have a wart.
13. You have dandruff.
14. You are in love with someone.
15. You think about getting married.
16. You are a bit lazy.
17. You feel you talk too much.
18. You secretly admire a person of the opposite sex.
19. You usually eat a good breakfast.
20. You enjoyed this game.

How Well Do You Know Your Wife?

1. What is her favorite color?
2. Name a food she can't stand.
3. How much sugar does she take in her coffee?
4. Does she squeeze the toothpaste from the bottom or from the middle?
5. Name two of her best friends.
6. What is her favorite food?
7. Would she rather spend a quiet evening at home or go out?
8. What part of the chicken does she like best?
9. How did she vote in the last election? for president? for governor?
10. What does she do when she has spare time?
11. What is her favorite flower?
12. Is she good at math?
13. How old was she when you married her?
14. What kind of noise irritates her the most?
15. If she had $25 to spend, what would she buy?

Singing Partners

The names of familiar songs are written on duplicate slips. One slip is given to a boy and the other to a girl. At a signal from the leader or hostess, all start singing or whistling their songs. This mixer will create a lot of noise as well as fun. When partners are found, the singing stops.

Chewing Gum Relay

Give each team a ladies' handbag in which there is a small folded paper bag and inside of that several fully wrapped sticks of gum. The first person is handed a pair of canvas gloves. On a signal this person puts on the gloves, opens the bag, gets one stick of the chewing gum, chews it, and whistles before passing on the bag to the next person, who repeats the pattern.

Impromptu Stories

Cut a dozen headlines out of the newspaper, or take large captions out of a magazine. Then cut out each individual word. Jumble all the words together, and, picking them out at random, give three different words to each player present. Each must then make up a story, using the three words given him to form the plot of the story. The person distributing the words should announce that the story is to be short and funny.

Drivers

Two or more teams are selected, each with two boys and a girl. The boys are blindfolded, and then they make a seat for the girl by each boy taking hold of his right wrist with his left hand and taking hold of the left wrist of the other boy with his right hand. The girl is then seated and all three are turned around two or three times so that the boys will lose their sense of direction. The signal to start is given and they must race to a goal and back, the blindfolded boys being guided by the girl who directs them. This will make many funny situations. It will probably create enough interest to have a second race with new teams after the first has been completed.

Noah's Ark

At the beginning of the game each girl is asked to select a partner. This may be done in any number of ways. After the group has been divided into couples, the leader names each couple, the idea being that they represent two of the animals that went into Noah's Ark. Animals should be selected which make a noise that can be imitated. There might be two horses, two hogs, two sheep, two cows, two chickens, two ducks, two turkeys, two frogs, and so on.

The boys now retire from the room and the girls change seats so as to confuse the boys when they return. The boys are blindfolded and led back into the room. Each girl immediately tries to attract her partner by making a noise which is made by the animal which she represents. The girls stand behind chairs and the boys are supposed to find the chair of their partner. This will be no easy matter because of the babble of sound. A prize might be given to the first one to find the proper chair, and a booby prize to the last one.

The game might be continued by having the girls retire and letting the boys imitate the animals.

Count to Thirty

Get eight or ten boys and eight or ten girls up in front of the group to "count to thirty." First the girls start, giving aloud a number, beginning with "one," and going from left to right (or starting wherever the leader points). The rule is that they must, instead of saying a numeral with a "seven" in it put palms together, and on a number divisible by seven, put hands together back to back (knuckles of center fingers touching). All other numbers are called aloud. Further rule: when one of these symbols has been given, the counting reverses in direction and goes down the line the opposite way. It is very hard to count to thirty.

Writing Games

Rumor Mill

While one player is out of the room, each of the others write a statement about him. The statements can be humorous, truthful, or ironical, but keep them kind. The statements are collected, the player returns, and one by one the statements are read to him. He then tries to identify the author of each statement. If he guesses one correctly, that author then takes his place.

180 Seconds

Give each person a piece of paper and a pencil. Tell them to list as many Bible characters as he/she can in 180 seconds (3 minutes). Give participants 180 seconds more to make couples out of the characters listed. Names may not be added to the list but a name may be used more than once.

Top Reporter

Write a topic on a slip of paper (example: Jesus Feeding 5,000; Israelites Crossing Red Sea, Paul Imprisoned, etc.) and place the slips in a box. Divide the group into couples and give each couple a piece of paper and a pencil. Each couple draws a topic from the box and then composes a headline and story on the topic.

Example: **Topic:** Israelites Crossing Red Sea

Headline: Red Sea Becomes Largest Cemetery in Existence

Story: The mighty Red Sea has become a cemetery for the powerful Egyptian army. A strong hurricane-level wind blew from heaven last night and divided the waters of the sea. The children of Israel walked across the sea on dry land. But when the Egyptian army pursued them, the great walls of water collapsed and drowned the entire battalion. An eyewitness said, "There was not one survivor." This is the worst disaster ever to come upon the Egyptian army. Moses and the children of Israel walked away from the terrible site singing and praising their God. It is reported that not one of the Israelites had mud on his sandles.

Give couples a time limit to prepare their report. Alternatives would be for each couple to select the topic they would like to report on, or assign a topic from the last five lessons studied.

Eye Color

Teen-agers will enjoy this game. Give each one a piece of paper and a pencil with the instruction of listing everyone that is present and the color of their eyes — without looking. Compare lists to see who is the most observant.

Animal Descriptions

As your guests arrive, give each a blank card and ask that they write their initials on it. After all the guests have done this, they are to exchange cards with the person nearest them. Each one is to then write the name of an animal that begins with the last initial. Two descriptive words are to be written beginning with the first two initials. For instance, T.E.M. could have "tall egotistical moose." The cards are then returned to the person whose initials they bear and are read aloud.

Artist

Choose a boy and a girl and place them back-to-back in chairs. The boy is given paper, pencil, and something firm to draw on. The girl is given an object. She must describe the object to the boy and he must draw it. The art and object are then compared to judge the results.

I'm a Number-One-Sniffer

Fill ten to twelve small containers with liquids and number each container. Give each player a card and a pencil, and have them number the cards according to the number of liquids. Starting with the container labeled "1," walk around the room and allow each player to quickly sniff it and immediately write down what he thinks that container holds. Possible liquids include: water, tea, coffee, Coke, Dr. Pepper, vinegar, ammonia, cough syrup, and vanilla. The one who correctly names the most liquids is the winner.

Walnut Chest

Take the shell of a walnut and put as many objects into it as possible. Tape the two halves together. Give the players a piece of paper and a pencil. Hold up the walnut. Tell the players exactly how many objects the walnut contains. Ask them to write a list of items the walnut possibly holds. Open the walnut and name the objects. The person who correctly guesses the most items is the winner. Possible objects include: a bean, rice, a kernel of corn, a hair, a piece of string, and a bit of eraser.

Observation

About twenty objects are placed on a table and covered with a cloth. Each player receives a piece of paper and a pencil. All players gather around the table and the cloth is removed. The players are given one minute to examine the objects before they are covered again. The players then list as many objects as they can remember. One point is scored for each object correctly listed and two points deducted for each object listed not found on the table.

Do You Know Your Advertisements?

Decorate your walls with different advertisements cut from magazines and newspapers. All the advertisements should be numbered and the name of the item cut from the advertisement. The guests are all given a piece of paper and a pencil and told to look at the wall decor. They are to list the names of the advertisements they recognize according to the way they are numbered. The one with the most correct should be given a prize.

Problems and Solutions

Give each person two slips of paper. They are to write a problem on one slip and a solution to any problem on the other. Collect all the problems in one box and solutions in another. Mix up the slips in each box. Then let each person draw one problem and one solution. They are to read aloud their problem and its solution.

Name Game

Supply a name and have the players write it down. Then instruct them to find names that begin with each letter of that name, and to write them down below the proper letter. No names may be duplicated. The players receive one point per letter used, so the object of the game is to use long names. The player with the most points wins the game. Set a time limit.

Example:

```
T H O M A S
H A L A B A
A R I R R M
D O V T A U
D L E H H E
E D R A A L
U       M
S
```

Famous Names

The following phrases suggest famous names. Give a copy to each guest and allow them a few moments to supply the answers. You may add names.

	Answers
1. A cherry tree	George Washington
2. A good thief	Robin Hood
3. A slingshot	David
4. An awakening kiss	Sleeping Beauty
5. A shattering fall	Humpty Dumpty
6. A burning bush	Moses
7. A glass slipper	Cinderella
8. A wicked kiss	Judas
9. A roaring pillow	Daniel
10. A new light	Thomas Edison
11. A new world	Columbus

Hidden Names

Find the hidden names in the statements below.

1.	A tree cemetery is a sight.	Reece
2.	Tomorrow evening.	Tom, Eve
3.	I dare you.	Ida
4.	Tan always matches brown.	Tana
5.	The cat is a small animal.	Lani, Al
6.	January's gone.	Jan
7.	He's a billionaire.	Bill
8.	It's only a sample.	Sam
9.	Do ugly people get rich?	Doug, Rich
10.	Frankly, I say no.	Frank
11.	The tavern on Hwy. 171.	Vernon
12.	A case of red apples.	Fred, Les
13.	The mandolin dates way back.	Linda
14.	Close the door, please.	Seth
15.	Bet he'll love to come.	Beth

State Game

The abbreviation of a state supplies the answer to the following descriptions.

	Answers
1. A president's name	Cal. — California
2. Most egotistical	Me. — Maine
3. A father	Pa. — Pennsylvania
4. A maiden	Miss. — Mississippi
5. Not healthy	Ill. — Illinois
6. A number	Tenn. — Tennessee

	Answers
7. Does not fail	Kan.—Kansas
8. Cutting grass	Mo.—Missouri
9. Noah's safety	Ark.—Arkansas
10. Produces metal	Ore.—Oregon
11. Exclamation	Oh.—Ohio
12. A girl's name	Minn.—Minnesota
13. Like a valley	Del.—Delaware
14. A clean state	Wash.—Washington
15. The sixth tone of the scale	La.—Louisiana
16. Cures the sick	Md.—Maryland

"B" Game

		Answers
1. B and one letter;	to exist.	Be
2. B and two letters;	a sack.	Bag
3. B and three letters;	a storehouse.	Barn
4. B and three letters;	a young creature.	Baby
5. B and three letters;	without hair.	Bald
6. B and three letters;	a vegetable.	Bean or Beet
7. B and three letters;	a drink.	Beer
8. B and three letters;	a part of a bird.	Beak
9. B and three letters;	a vessel.	Boat
10. B and four letters;	a tree.	Birch
11. B and four letters;	to commence.	Begin
12. B and four letters;	a kind of meat.	Bacon
13. B and five letters;	a combat.	Battle
14. B and five letters;	a hound.	Beagle
15. B and five letters;	a signal.	Beacon

51

"For" Game

The first syllable of each answer begins with <u>for</u>. Complete the names.

1.	From another country	<u>for</u> eign
2.	Many trees	<u>for</u> est
3.	Always	<u>for</u> ever
4.	To give up	<u>for</u> feit
5.	Loss of memory	<u>for</u> get
6.	Not casual	<u>for</u> mal
7.	Army post	<u>for</u> t
8.	Plans	<u>for</u> mat
9.	To insist	<u>for</u> ce
10.	To restrict	<u>for</u> bid

"Bar" Game

1.	Uncivilized	<u>bar</u> barian
2.	Uncover	<u>bar</u> e
3.	Hair cutter	<u>bar</u> ber
4.	Towed by a tugboat	<u>bar</u> ge
5.	Musical sound	<u>bar</u> itone
6.	Doggy talk	<u>bar</u> k
7.	No saddle	<u>bar</u> eback
8.	No children	<u>bar</u> ren
9.	Large round container	<u>bar</u> rel
10.	Blocking wall	<u>bar</u> rier

"Man" Game

1. Store boss — man ager _____
2. Musical instrument — man dolin _____
3. Crazy person — man iac _____
4. Jesus' bed — man ger _____
5. Food from God — man na _____
6. Store dummy — man nequin _____
7. Beautiful home — man sion _____
8. Over fireplaces — man tel _____
9. Horses' hair — man e _____
10. More than one — man y _____

Girls' Names

Find the name that matches the clue. Put the number by the correct name.

1. Ring-a-ling	9	Susan
2. Easter flower	6	Ruby
3. Clear, transparent	10	Nell
4. Climbing flower	1	Belle
5. Day before	8	Sherry
6. Blood red	3	Crystal
7. Oyster produce	2	Lilly
8. Alcoholic beverage	4	Rose
9. A lazy flower	7	Pearl
10. Mournful sound	5	Eve

Boys' Names

Follow instructions given in game above.

1. Drop-off, ledge	5	Frank
2. Pay each month	10	Adam
3. Cut off short	7	Mike
4. Scribble	9	Ray
5. Straightforward	1	Cliff
6. Absorbent towel	3	Bob
7. Speak into	8	Jack
8. Type of rabbit	2	Bill
9. Sun gives off	6	Terry
10. First man	4	Mark

Bible Characters

Match the man to his wife and child.

Father	Mother		Child	
1. Abraham	Hannah	4	Obed	8
2. Isaac	Ahinoam	7	Jesus	10
3. Jacob	Mary	10	Seth	5
4. Elkanah	Sarah	1	John	9
5. Adam	Elizabeth	9	Isaac	1
6. David	Rebekah	2	Samuel	4
7. Saul	Rachel	3	Jacob	2
8. Boaz	Eve	5	Solomon	6
9. Zacharias	Bathsheba	6	Joseph	3
10. Joseph	Ruth	8	Jonathan	7

Men of the Bible

Unscramble these names:

Anho	Noah	Vaidd	David	Veil	Levi
Sjseu	Jesus	Lendia	Daniel	Doreh	Herod
Anaor	Aaron	Mhoats	Thomas	Ertpe	Peter
Pula	Paul	Llihppi	Phillip	Sseom	Moses
Jdue	Jude	Amda	Adam		

Women in the Bible

Unscramble these names.

Zebjeel	Jezebel	Soil	Lois	Rasha	Sarah
Nanahh	Hannah	Nueeci	Eunice	Ordcas	Dorcas
Yram	Mary	Doarh	Rhoda	Thru	Ruth
Vee	Eve	Heal	Leah	Imoan	Naomi
Yadil	Lydia	Chrael	Rachel	Hatarm	Martha

Trees

Unscramble these names.

koa	oak	ucespr	spruce
gif	fig	nolmagia	magnolia
erap	pear	ppale	apple
edarc	cedar	cepan	pecan
nipe	pine	moresyca	sycamore
eampl	maple	deroowd	redwood
mapl	palm	godoodw	dogwood
rif	fir		

Cities

Unscramble these names.

Sajemelur	Jerusalem	Sarpi	Paris
Wne Kyor	New York	Tonhous	Houston
Wne Leorans	New Orleans	Lldasa	Dallas
Llyohoowd	Hollywood	Sobnot	Boston
Bileom	Mobile	Sawhingnot	Washington
Verden	Denver	Peohxin	Phoenix
Eillvhasn	Nashville	Sonjack	Jackson
Linber	Berlin		

Animals

Unscramble these names.

xfo	fox	tgao	goat	tnetki	kitten
afcl	calf	epehs	sheep	noil	lion
oosrtre	rooster	kynode	donkey	bzera	zebra
goh	hog	kienchc	chicken	phelante	elephant
eulm	mule	lubl	bull	terpanh	panther

Flowers

Unscramble these names.

sore	rose	agmnolia	magnolia
letiov	violet	zaalea	azalea
dihcor	orchid	arnaction	carnation
pulit	tulip	liyl	lily
rsii	iris	dineagar	gardenia
macelia	camelia	aisyd	daisy
ewest ape	sweet pea	eerpc yrtlem	crepe myrtle

Fish

Unscramble these names.

rtout	trout	sabs	bass
naut	tuna	tachisf	catfish
barc	crab	rimshp	shrimp
stolerb	lobster	syoter	oyster
dre nppaser	red snapper	mansol	salmon

States

Give each player a pencil and paper. Allow ten minutes for the players to write as many states and capitals as they can remember. Five points are given for each state and ten points for each capital. Fifteen points are deducted for every mistake.

Water

Give each player a pencil and paper. Allow ten minutes for the players to list as many bodies of water in or touching the borders of the United States as they can. The players score twenty points for every ocean and gulf, fifteen points for every river, ten points for every lake, and five points for every creek or bayou.

Your Name

Give each player a pencil and paper. Allow ten minutes for him to write as many words as he can get out of his own name. He may not repeat letters. For every three-letter word he gets five points; four-letter words, ten points; and five-letter (or more) words, fifteen points.

Rectangle

The following names of Bible men are found in the word rectangle. The names may be found vertically, diagonally, or horizontally. Some names are found in reverse and some letters are used more than once. Circle each name.

Aaron	Benjamin	Hur	Matthew
Abimelech	Boaz	Isaac	Naaman
Absalom	Cain	Isaiah	Nebuchadnezzar
Adam	Cyrus	Jacob	Omri
Ahaz	Dan	James	Pilate
Ahi	David	Jeremiah	Pul
Amos	Eli	Joel	Samuel
Amram	Enoch	Joseph	Seth
Arad	Esau	Lamech	Silas
Asa	Ezra	Levi	Simon
Asher	Felix	Lot	Terah
Baal	Gad	Luke	Timothy
Balaam	Ham	Malachi	Uriah
Barnabas	Hezekiah	Mark	Zur

Christmas

Find these words in the puzzle.

Savior	peace	baby
manger	love	noel
Christ	tax	stable
carol	hay	Mary
Jesus	trees	angels
joy	ornament	gift

```
R U H E Z E K I A H I I E B
A M R A M L L E U M A S M A
Z A C M H E U S D F H A A R
Z T H U A V P E I E A I L N
E T C M I I O T V L Z A A A
N H O O M R I H A I U H C B
D E N L E O J B D X R A H A
A W E A R Z E E I N O M I S
H M S S E N G S U R Y C O I
C A J B J B A A L H A J N L
U R I A H A D U T I J A A A
B K M N C A A O N O A M O S
E I U O N O M U S M E E Z H
N D A R A I B E A C K S A E
P I L A T E P N H U O Z O R
T E R A H H C E L E M I B A
```

```
T R E E S X P L M O
O X R M A N G E R R
H A Y A V P L E O N
S T W R I Z B W C A
O T E Y O A C A S M
T Y A O R S R T O E
S O N B L O V E R N
I J G E L G I F T T
R A E O P E Y B A B
H O L P E A C E E R
C A S A R S U S E J
```

Women

Follow the instructions given for the preceding game.

Abi	Abigail	Adah	Anna
Deborah	Esther	Eve	Gomer
Hagar	Hannah	Herodias	Jael
Jezebel	Jochebed	Leah	Lois
Lydia	Martha	Mary	Miriam
Orpah	Priscilla	Rahab	Ruth
Sarah	Shua	Vashti	Zilpah
Zipporah			

```
Z  O  A  B  I  G  A  I  L  U
Z  I  P  V  A  S  R  E  R  S
H  A  P  R  O  E  A  E  I  H
A  L  R  P  H  H  M  Z  A  U
R  B  I  T  O  O  Y  G  D  A
O  J  S  V  G  R  A  H  A  B
B  E  C  H  A  R  A  S  H  Z
E  A  I  M  O  V  M  H  L  D
D  H  L  O  O  I  A  E  V  E
L  T  L  B  R  N  A  R  A  B
O  R  A  I  N  J  I  O  S  E
I  A  A  A  G  A  D  D  H  H
S  M  H  T  U  R  Y  I  T  C
J  E  Z  E  B  E  L  A  I  O
H  H  A  P  L  I  Z  S  L  J
```

Smarts

Have each player draw a chart like the one below. The leader chooses a word to be written across the top and four categories to be placed on the side. The players are to fill in each square with a word that begins with the letter at the top of the column and falls into the category at the left. Five points are given for each successful word. A time limit of five minutes should be set.

	M	O	T	H	E	R
City	Memphis	Omaha	Trenton	Houston	El Paso	Ragley
State	Miss.	Ohio	Tenn.	Hawaii	X	Rhode Island
Girl's Name	Melba	Opal	Teresa	Hazel	Eva	Rowena
Boy's Name	Mark	Omar	Tim	Harold	Ed	Richey

Animals

Give each player a pencil and paper containing a list of animals. They are to write the name of the male, female, and offspring of each. Below are some you may wish to use.

	Male	Female	Offspring
Horse	Stallion	Mare	Foal
Hog	Boar	Sow	Pig
Cat	Tom	Minnie	Kitten
Goat	Billy	Nanny	Kid
Deer	Buck	Doe	Fawn
Chicken	Rooster	Hen	Chick
Donkey	Jack	Jenny	Foal
Fox	Dog	Fox	Vixen
Dog	Dog	Gip	Pup
Goose	Gander	Goose	Gosling

Find Your Twin

The leader gives each person a sheet as follows:

Find Your Twin
Time Limit: 10 minutes

	Yours	Get Autograph of Twin
1. Color of eyes	_____	_____
2. Favorite hobby	_____	_____
3. Color of hair	_____	_____
4. Shoe size	_____	_____
5. Favorite food	_____	_____
6. Favorite color	_____	_____
7. Number of subjects at school	_____	_____
8. Favorite drink	_____	_____
9. Dress size or jean size	_____	_____
10. Kind of pet	_____	_____

Names

Give each player a piece of paper and a pencil. Instruct them to number the paper vertically from one to twenty-six and to list the letters of the alphabet vertically alongside the numbers. Then give the name of a song, old proverb, or title of a book and have them write it vertically down the paper, one letter per line. Don't worry if the proverb is too long, however provide extra letters if it is too short. Then give the players a few minutes to think of people who have the initials of the letters on each line. The players may not make up fictitious names. The player with the most names is the winner.

Couples

Below are listed ten men and women who are or were at one time married. Can you match them?

Answers

		Answers
1. George	A. Elizabeth	1. D
2. Eddie	B. Joan	2. E
3. Ronald	C. Jackie	3. H
4. Richard	D. Martha	4. A
5. Abraham	E. Debbie	5. J
6. John	F. Ethel	6. C
7. Robert	G. Mamie	7. F
8. Charles	H. Nancy	8. I
9. Ted	I. Diana	9. B
10. Dwight	J. Sarah	10. G

History

Can you match the incident, title, or occupation to the correct person or group?

		Answers
1. Boston Tea Party	A. Al Capone	1. D
2. Outlaw	B. Robert E. Lee	2. F
3. Discoverer	C. Zac Taylor	3. I
4. President	D. Colonists	4. C
5. Mafia	E. Thomas Edison	5. A
6. General	F. Jesse James	6. B
7. Baseball player	G. Mexicans	7. J
8. Alamo	H. Miners	8. G
9. Gold Rush	I. Sir Walter Raleigh	9. H
10. Inventor	J. Babe Ruth	10. E

Bible Mistakes

Supply the group with paper and pencils. Have someone read a well-known Bible incident, supplying some incorrect names, places, numbers, or incidents throughout. See who can list the most mistakes.

Telegrams

Give each player a piece of paper and a pencil. Instruct them to write a certain word across the top of the paper such as Christmas, Halloween, or Easter. Then have them write a telegram using each letter of the word, for instance, Easter: *E*very *a*unt *s*ends *t*hanks, *e*ven *R*uth.

Shopping Spree

Place the objects listed in the second column on a table. Give participants the numbered list and ask them to "purchase" the objects by listing the item next to the correct clue.

Clue	Object
1. Hidden tears	Onion
2. Bygone days	Last year's calendar
3. A drive through the wood	A nail in a block
4. We part to meet again	A pair of shears
5. Tax on tea	Some tacks on a box of tea
6. Home of Burns	Electric iron
7. The greatest bet ever made	Alphabet
8. Way-worn traveler	An old shoe
9. My own native land	Small pile of dirt
10. House the Colonel lived in	English walnut hull
11. Light of other days	A candle

12. Ruins of China	Broken dish
13. Broken heart	A candy heart, broken
14. Sweet sixteen	Sixteen pieces of candy
15. The four seasons	Four spices
16. A line from home	A clothes line
17. Kids at rest	Kid gloves
18. A perfect foot	12-inch ruler
19. Something to adore	A key or doorknob
20. Something that can't be beat	Hard-boiled egg
21. Olivet	An olive seed
22. The horse fair	Oats
23. The world's fair	Pictures of girls
24. A book that is never read	A blue, green, or yellow book
25. One that is going to be licked	A lollipop

You Name the Offspring

The leader prepares typewritten or mimeographed sheets for each guest with the following names typed on them. The name of the offspring is left blank, and the guests, working either singly or in pairs, fill in the name of the offspring which these couples might have.

Mr. and Mrs. Mite	Dina (dynamite)
Mr. and Mrs. Rot	Tommy (tommyrot)
Mr. and Mrs. Board	Bill (billboard)
Mr. and Mrs. Mander	Jerry (gerrymander)
Mr. and Mrs. Tock	Matt (mattock)
Mr. and Mrs. Anthemum	Cris (chrysanthemum)
Mr. and Mrs. Itosis	Hal (halitosis)

Mr. and Mrs. Iculate	Art (articulate)
Mr. and Mrs. Fi	Terry (terrify)
Mr. and Mrs. Mire	Ad (admire)
Mr. and Mrs. Vere	Percy (persevere)
Mr. and Mrs. Tor	Eddie (editor)
Mr. and Mrs. Tate	Hessie (hesitate)
Mr. and Mrs. Nasium	Jim (gymnasium)
Mr. and Mrs. Ware	Bee (beware)
Mr. and Mrs. Tastic	Fan (fantastic)
Mr. and Mrs. Tant	Milly (militant)
Mr. and Mrs. Grant	Emmy (emigrant)
Mr. and Mrs. Quill	John (jonquil)
Mr. and Mrs. Ficial	Benny (beneficial)
Mr. and Mrs. Mum	Minnie (minimum)

This game is also good as an oral quiz. The leader might read the family names and ask the guests to hold up their hands if they are able to give the name of the offspring.

The guest can probably think of a number of other names to add to his list, and the leader may ask the guests to make suggestions.

Banquet Games
and Skits

The Serenaders

Make a list of all who will attend and choose a song (or parts of a song) that will fit each person. You will have to change some of the words. As the guests sit at their tables, have someone stroll around, call out names, and serenade them. A guitar player/singer would be ideal, but an accordian or piano will suffice.

> Example: Lori—Amazing love, how could it be, to think
> that Craig could really care for thee ...
> Allan—Baby face, you got the cutest little baby
> face ...

You should include every member of your group.

The Gossip Skit

Compile a list of all who will attend the banquet and make up some gossip about each. For the skit have an old lady sitting as another (Zelda) comes to the door. The old lady invites Zelda in and they talk about good things just for a few seconds. Then, "Zelda, far be it from me to gossip, but do you know what I heard just today? ..." Have the old lady tell Zelda all the things you have made up about the guests, using their names and filling the conversation with "Girl, don't you dare use my name if you should repeat this," "Now you know I'm not one for gossiping," "Girl, don't you breathe a word of this to anyone," etc. When the visitor starts to depart the old lady says: "Zelda, I must go, Lord bless you honey, and don't dare use my name if you should pass this on." After she leaves Zelda picks up the phone, calls several people, and tells them all the stories (mix up the names and details) using the older lady's name often. (It is very humorous to write about the pastor preaching about gossip Wednesday night and you just can't figure out who the guilty person is and why would anyone want to gossip—don't they know that's wrong. You wished you knew who the guilty one was so you could talk to them and maybe help them.)

This can be hilarous. Be sure to include all the members of the group. You can combine two or three in one story.

The Private Eye

Make a list of all who will attend. Write a little story about each or describe them in a humorous way. Let the guests guess who you are talking about.

> Example: He has burned rubber on every highway in northeast Louisiana. The demons must chase him each night, for there could be no other reason one would drive so fast.

Santa Claus Is Coming to Town

Find someone to dress up as Santa Claus or as one of his helpers. Get a group of teens together. Have Santa come in and hand out gifts accompanied by witty or poetic sayings. Santa may, for example, hand out a large plastic key and say,

> Jeff, here's the key to Sue's heart.
> Could it be you were meant for each other
> right from the start?

Mannequins

This is a skit requiring four or five people. It's after closing hours in a department store and two janitors have come in to clean. Several people are posed an mannequins. Fill the skit with antics. For example, a janitor may turn his back to a mannequin and it kicks him. That janitor accuses the other janitor and so on. The janitors finally realize that neither has touched the other. They run from the room spooked.

The Quizzers Panel Contest

Choose three to five people to be on a panel. Place a bell in front of each. The leader then asks a question. The first person to ring his bell may answer the question. Have a comprehensive list of questions concerning history, math, science, literature, and the Bible. Keep score.

Sales Pitch

Send three people out. Bring in one at a time blindfolded. Give him a serving tray to hold with a roll of toilet tissue on top. Tell him he must use his best sales pitch to sell this unknown object to everyone.

The Incredible Eating Machine

Have several people sit under a sheet with the eyes of one person showing through holes in the sheet. Also have a large hole for its mouth. Someone talks to and feeds the monster to pacify him. He gives him a can of Coke and someone under the sheet immediately throws out an empty can. He gives him a banana and someone throws out a peel. This may continue for as long as you wish, but the last item given to the monster is a baby doll. Someone under the sheet holds the baby and throws out clothes identical to what the doll is wearing. The monster wobbles out of the room with the doll.

Class of 1930

Get some older adults to act out what it was like to be in high school in 1930 (or 1940 or 1950). Have them dress to fit the part of a football player, cheerleader, schoolgirl, and so on. They could possibly sing songs from that time.

Contagious

The setting is a doctor's office. A receptionist is answering telephone calls when a man comes in to see the doctor. She takes his name and address and asks what his problem is. He tells her that he catches every disease and ailment that he comes in contact with. He takes a seat. A second person comes in and tells the receptionist that he has a bad cough. He takes a seat and begins to cough. The first man begins to cough. A third person comes in with a bad itch followed by someone with a twitch. A fifth person comes in with a dislocated shoulder, and a sixth has a leg that uncontrollably kicks. The first person takes on the ailment of each person that walks in: he coughs, scratches, twitches, moves shoulder, and kicks his leg uncontrollably. Finally a pregnant woman walks in. The man gets bug-eyed, jumps up, and runs out of the office.

Twelve Days of Christmas

Get someone to sing this song. Pause after each to let one or more stand and imitate that gift.

Love

A couple dressed as an old man and woman walk in and sit in rockers. The old woman embroiders while the old man reads the paper. A young couple stroll by holding hands, obviously in love. The old woman looks at them with remembrance in her eyes. She gets her compact out of her apron pocket and powders her nose, combs her hair, and applies lipstick. She then says, "Honey, you don't ever sit next to me like you used to." He puts his horn to his ear and says, "Huh?" She repeats it. He pulls his chair next to hers and continues to read. Then she says, "Honey, you don't ever put your arm around me anymore." He again puts the horn to his ear and says, "Huh?" She says it again and he slowly puts his arm around her. Finally she says, "Honey, you don't ever nibble on my ear like you used to." He puts the horn up to his ear and she again repeats her words. He slowly gets up and starts to leave. She says, "Where are you going, honey?" He replies, "Gotta get my teeth."

Graduation

For all the honored graduates you need a "This Is Your Life" reading. Have someone research and compose a reading on each graduate starting with their birth through present.

Mimicry

If the crowd varies in age, have a young person mimic an older one and an older one mimic a teenager. The audience is to guess who is being mimicked in each case. For each person being mimicked, think of something funny that happened to that person, or of a peculiar quirk or habit that he has (humming, clearing his throat, pushing on nosepiece of glasses, etc.). Do not be unkind or offensive.

Guess Who

This works well for small banquets. Obtain a baby picture from everyone that will attend. Attach each picture to a backing. At the banquet pass the pictures so that everyone gets to see all of them. The pictures may be numbered and paper and pencil given so that guesses may be recorded. Then go through the pictures and have each person stand when you come to his or her picture.

Hillbilly Wedding

This can be a fun performance if you can find some witty people to play the parts. The setting is a hillbilly wedding. The hillbillies wear old, patched, and mismatched clothes and talk in hillbilly slang. The wedding ceremony should be full of interruptions such as crying, arguments, and perhaps even a few songs. Pa should have a shotgun, the groom should be handcuffed, and ma should have plenty of handkerchiefs.